Sightline

Sightline

ELIZABETH AUSTEN

ANDREA BATES

CAROL STEVENS KNER

SARAH SUZOR

poems

toadlily press
chappaqua, ny

Toadlily Press
P.O. Box 2, Chappaqua, NY 10514
www.toadlilypress.com

Cover Art from *Window Light* by Charlotte Brieff
Book Design by Liz Lester

The following poems have appeared in the cited publications:

"Against the Hegemony of Lawn Grass" *The Common Ground Review*
"Consume" *A Trunk of Delirium*
"False Spring" *DMQ Review*
"Heavenly Rest" *Western Humanities Review*
"Her, at Two" *Willow Springs*
"Humans" *Crab Creek Review*
"In This Small Room" *California Quarterly*
"In Addition To" and "In Retrospect" *OR*
"Isle of Dogs" (first poem) *OR*
"L'Amour Fou, L'Amour Wild" *Cutthroat*
"It Didn't Happen That Way" *The Moment Witnessed, Poems from Poets of the
    Fifth Skagit River Poetry Festival*
"Leaving the Island" was commissioned for the Richard Hugo House Literary Series
"Loving Icarus" *Into the Teeth of the Wind*
"Masters of the Renaissance" *The Paris Review* and set to music by Carl Frank
    Smith at the Blair School of Music (a commission by Emory University)
"Overhead, Underfoot" *Bellingham Review*
"The Permanent Fragility of Meaning" *Poets Against the War* (Thunder's Mouth
    Press / Nation Books)
"V.I.P. Lounge" *Connecticut River Review*
"The Visit" set to music by Christopher Berg as part of a song cycle titled "Songs of
    Leisure"
"Where Currents Meet" *Bellingham Review*

Publication of this volume is made possible in part by individual contributions
and by a grant from the NY State Council on the Arts to Fractured Atlas on
behalf of Toadlily Press.

PUBLISHER'S CATALOGING-IN-PUBLICATION DATA
(Prepared by The Donohue Group, Inc.)

Sightline : poems / Elizabeth Austen . . . [et al.].
        p. ; cm. — (The Quartet series)
    A collection of poems written by Elizabeth Austen, Andrea Bates, Sarah
Suzor and Carol Stevens Kner.
    ISBN: 978-0-9766405-5-4
        1. American poetry—21st century. 2. Poetry—Women authors. I. Austen,
Elizabeth. II. Bates, Andrea. III. Suzor, Sarah. IV. Kner, Carol Stevens.
PS589.S54   2010
811.60809287   2010928412

CONTENTS

CAROL STEVENS KNER
Exposure

SARAH SUZOR
Isle of Dogs

FOREWORD

Gathered under the one title, *Sightline*, Elizabeth Austen, Andrea Bates, Carol Stevens Kner and Sarah Suzor add their highly individuated voices to a single point in time in contemporary American poetry.

These chapbooks join a storied history of a form produced by alternative presses like that of the 18th century bluestocking Hannah More, poet, philanthropist, and advocate for literacy. Along with her sisters and friends, More published over 100 titles in her Cheap Repository Tracts selling an unprecedented 2 million copies a year, making reading material accessible at a time when libraries were private and conventionally produced books prohibitively expensive.

Meredith Trede and Myrna Goodman are literary pioneers as well. As editors of Toadlily Press, they carve a place in the canon with a hybrid form of the chapbook, one that combines four short collections of poetry bound into one. They put into print, and therefore circulation, the work of four poets.

Compression serves as an innovative organizing principle in this four-part collection, creating an elevated sense that every poem is vital. The first collection, *Where Currents Meet*, opens with an epigraph, quoting Stanley Kunitz: "Out of our contradictions we build our harmonies." **Elizabeth Austen** slyly weaves contradictions into crafted poems haunted with questions. She builds elements of regret into poems that use blank space as a kind of caesura or pause in the line as in "Overhead, Underfoot":

> *sandpipers clean the beach, one*
> *flea at a time   the wrecked*
>
> *boat bleached anonymous   herons*
> *disperse like sentries along the tide line*

Her fine poems are followed by those of **Andrea Bates**, whose aptly named *Origami Heart* shapes a cautionary tale—that later-in-life love is not for the faint of heart. In one poem her amorous persona eyes a voyeur watching the speaker and a lover through an open window, and together they become connoisseurs of "the great escape of middle age." In "Sonnet of Homophones," she gathers the common threads of her work into an origami knot with "The past / is a tight corset worn by heroines / who cannot forget."

Sightline is full of discoveries, a signature element of the chapbook, and wonderfully so with **Sarah Suzor**'s *Isle of Dogs*. Suzor seems to channel Sappho in her lean modern-day poems, a narrative made up of fragments that expose a razor-sharp intelligence, an unnerving sophistication, an echo of poet Anne Carson. As in:

> *She said, I had never been here before.*
> *She had.*

And, in "Consume":

> *When something is distracting concentrate on its shadow.*

All four of these collections have a clearly defined arc. While Suzor's twelve poems build on each other, seamlessly linked as if one long poem, the others find a totem in one. **Carol Stevens Kner**'s collection, *Exposure*, culminates in a stunning poem, "Babblewacky," giving her poems a magical cohesion. The text, a word-meister's wonderland, draws language from an autopsy report. The poem is a remarkable ride on its sonic shapeliness. In six rhymed stanzas the poet offers up a "fiendish gimble of the brain" (a phrase from another poem), and repeats the first line of "Babblewacky" in the first line of the last stanza: "Invisible the senile plaques / growing stealthily like moss, / petrifying layers of chalk, / each tangled gain, another loss."

The Quartet chapbook series presents just enough work by each poet for the reader to get a solid sense of each writer's poetry, and leaves us wanting more!

Elaine Sexton
New York City, June 2010

Where Currents Meet

ELIZABETH AUSTEN

Out of our contradictions we build our harmonies.
STANLEY KUNITZ

The Permanent Fragility of Meaning

Why persist, scratching across the white field
row after row? Why repeat the ritual
every morning, emptying my hands
asking for a new prayer to fold
and unfold?

> Nothing changes, no one is saved.

I walk into the day, hands still
empty, and beg
to be of use to someone. I lie down
in the dark and beg to believe
when the voice comes again with its commands
with its promises—

> *unfold your hands. Revelation*
is not a fruit you pluck from trees. This is the work
cultivating the smallest shoot, readying your tongue
to shape the sacred names, your mouth already filling—

I lie down in the dark.

I rise up and begin again.

It Didn't Happen That Way

It wasn't a lure, dangled
by some fallen angel.
She found it, mid-path
no tree nearby. Unbruised
red-yellow round

sprung from the gravel.
She entered the sweet
fruit, wet flesh
breaking on her tongue. She didn't
ask for it. Wasn't
looking for it. No one

tempted her. Unless
the apple itself, longing
to be known, can be blamed
for the light bent
across its skin
for the mid-day heat
transforming sugar to scent.

And him? She didn't say
a word to him. He found her
slack-jawed, skin
flushed and damp
as if he had lain on her
pressed into her—

he found her, swallow by swallow
savoring the taste of knowledge
her eyes fixed, focused

somewhere beyond him
as if he no longer existed.
And one more thing—
she didn't tempt him. In fact
she never offered it.

He pried the fruit
from her hand, desperate
to follow, and bit.

Her, at Two

Sometimes a bone
at the tender back of the throat
requires a wracking, indelicate
cough to survive it. Sometimes
a bone is plucked—still

fully fleshed—
from the platter and brandished
like a baton, a magician's wand.
She transfixes every guest
gluttonous tyrant

in miniature. Is this how we all
began, thrilled to hold the meat
in our tiny fists, sure
the feast was laid for us
alone? Soon she will want

what she cannot reach
will be told it's not for her.
That's not lady-like.
Wipe your fingers.
Put down the bone.

Oh, let her be lucky
and rare, let it be years
before her sex is learned
as limitation, a fence
to circumscribe her life.

Before that verdict is delivered
let her travel so far
into her own skin
she'll shrug off that suit
of expectations, clothe

her mind according to her own
desires, bite the flesh
from the bone. I want
to be her and want
to have birthed her

and I want her
to survive. That girl—
who reaches and takes
erupts in glee as she shakes her fistful
of bone and meat.

Good-bye, My Millions

At twenty weeks' gestation, the peak of a female's
oogonial load, the fetus holds 6 to 7 million eggs.
NATALIE ANGIER, *Woman*

The husband will proffer but here's what he
offers: denatured, defused—a deliberate
blank. You cast in vain your thread of welcome
little debutante, pod of potential
packet of proteins and chromosomes.
You play to empty houses
on a darkened stage. No more
unto the breach, no more. Your gentleman
caller's all shine, no spark. His wallet holds
nothing but counterfeit notes. I know
you can't help it—your nature to ripen
and leap, linger by the phone for the call.
Invisible. Not viable. Again, as always
this scene must end in blood.

Humans

a brief and strange species
          W.S. MERWIN

the day begins in disarray   *you ought you should you must*
you must you must you must   the bees will not

be stilled   what stitches mind to body   who cues the unraveling
if it's true we're infused with something not found in doorknob bird

or bee why am I confused about all the important things   crows
trampoline the power lines from house to house   they don't care

who runs the world   I gape at the sky   color of sunflower
color of blood   the world is not as I have believed it to be

I find no vantage point   no long view across even the surface
peristalsis propels the worm into darkness   electricity

animates the lamp   the leaf drinks at the top of the tree
I understand none of the beautiful things   the sparrow bathes

in dirt   I don't know why   the birds do not ask themselves
or each other *how are we to live*   they do not ask us to love them

Overhead, Underfoot

Useless Bay, Whidbey Island

sandpipers clean the beach, one
flea at a time   the wrecked

boat bleached anonymous   herons
disperse like sentries along the tide line

tail without its rabbit   a fortune
in sand dollars   twice each day

the sea pretends to give back
what it takes   I walk from here to there

here to elsewhere   scraps float
across the marsh   *once was lost*

blind but now   are you hiding
or are you always on the move   a flock

of terns, scattering, gathering
shifting wordless on the wind

A Moment Ago

nothing happened
the couch still green   the month
still February   every chair

presses the carpet with the same
shape and force   nothing happened

we each wear
the same face still
breathe   that tonnage

of kindling our voices
felled split peeled and stacked
a moment ago   nothing

happened   still
every floorboard

listens   waits
for the match flare
not possible until—

Leaving the Island

ferry from Orcas to Anacortes

We carry what we found, what we made there.
Mist-colored knots of sea glass. A moss-clot

cadged from the trail's edge. The truce
fished word by word from beneath the surface

but still unspoken. Three days you and I
let the currents direct our course, we slept

on cool sand and let woodsmoke flavor us.
What's left? Slow travel over cold water.

Toward home and days ordered by clocks
instead of tides. We watch through salt-scarred

windows, hoping the dark shapes will rise
beside us, will grace us. We know too well

what cannot be willed, only missed
if we look away too soon.

False Spring

Frost, again, brittles the grass
darkens the reckless bud.

Our breaths: a kind of weather
we make between us, partly cloudy.
We skirt the pond's icy cap—

eyeing the single glove, its handless
caress, frozen against a branch.

Shi Shi Beach

Seagulls spread like a gray and white
beach towel abandoned

below the tide line.
My face hot with new sunburn

shoulders and hips buoyant
now the pack is set aside, the tent

assembled. My eyes rest
on the horizon, the seam

between ocean and air
unravels and shadows gather

in the forest at my back.
Shi Shi arcs northward, lets

the receding tide carry its pebbles
and the day's bootprints away.

I need this
like some people need

money or children or certainty—
to travel naked into an evening ocean

water rising with its own
irresistible rhythm, the chill

taking the soft place behind each knee
cresting my hips as my fingers trail

in the slow current. I come here alone
to find with my feet

and whatever momentum I can gather
how deep it might go

how much
can be immersed and retrieved

and immersed.

Where Currents Meet

Cattle Point, San Juan Island

See? Even at slack water a churn
of contradictions. Stay back, instinct

instructs. But from here, more beauty than danger.
Water is its own gravity, light

itself a lure. Lean in to the patterned
motion, ripples to the north, standing waves

to the south, the steady shove—
toward what? Chaos that comforts? Nothing here

is expected to make sense—contrary
intentions, even the charts

predict this. An improvisation
under the surface, revealed

by the interplay of light: water
with texture. Whatever invites attention

prayer enough for now. You could wait your whole
life for sense to take shape. Does it matter

from here, whether those are seals or
bull kelp? Keep looking.

Origami Heart

ANDREA BATES

Fretwork

My spine is your ornamental design,
see how the vertebrae recline or play,
vibrate to your indexed desire. You stay,
handle the handle of me, then unwind

me into the movie of darkness where
the bed is always unmade. I wait for
you to see through me, x-ray the bones, more
signs of heatstroke, love's overdose. A dare

to feel me through blank spaces, bend the air
between my toes, hold me until I'm gone,
the moons of my eyelids levitate bone,
eaves of my ears echo and reverb where

every stringed note you pull, pitch and woo,
kisses my neck, lingering long and blue.

L'Amour Fou, L'Amour Wild

You will do foolish things, but do them with enthusiasm.
SIDONIE GABRIELLE COLETTE

C'est la vie. Love is eternal while it lasts.
And so you recommend a tonic of raw rapture,
indigo jazz stippling air, saxophone notes,
goblets of cabernet, chivalry routed from the sofa,

last elegies to charities for the blind: it's time
his eyes wheeled the spin of your destruction,
silk-robed and unwinding thread by thread, no
immunity to what isn't good for you—or whom.

Pour yourself another glass, the boy is nervous.
Words to reassure: there is no east or west,
all is human in its naturalness, never say:
I could be your mother by the way. It ruins

the moment when he discovers the legend,
atlas to your city within a city where florists
sell blood orchids and crosswalks ribbon
your thighs. First, try love on for size:

the moment he kneels to anoint the goddess,
open the gates of his hands in the darkness,
let him flood your body with his sweetness,
nature's steady hum, air pleasured with love

sounds. Fig trees rustle and bees savor nectar
kisses that rosette his skin. The real you hidden
behind eyelids, flowered fields where a girl still
runs naked, on fire, *l'amour fou, l'amour wild.*

Against the Hegemony of Lawn Grass

If a man walking in the fields find any four-leaved grass, he shall in a small while after find some good thing.

SIR JOHN MELTON

Lay me down in a bed of clover,
bed me beside the bee who combs
for sweetness in downy fields, like us,
who buzz and swoon, open and ripe
one afternoon to what has plucked
us from unlucky destiny and placed
us here, where we belong to only each
other and the green we make of song,
of bee, of lust and its symphony, trefoils
that rustle beneath our hips and bees
that dip their wings into petals of deep
replenishing, a sweetness too long soured
by weeds devouring what we now reclaim,
what we release, in this time, in this hour.

In This Small Room

What I have wanted
in this small room
in these small hours
a spray of gardenias
a carpet of garments
all silks and sheens and cottons
all the dappled stretch of you
the frescoed cluster of your hair
the nest for my lips to come home to
and you, running your fingers
down my spine,
leaving your colors there.

View from a Mirror: Couple Kissing

Photograph by Brassai, Paris, 1932

A mirror is an eye that frames a lover's kiss.
Lipstick imprints cigarettes, ashtray by the bed.
A lover is a man who freely shares his bliss.

It always comes to this: smoke's misty genesis.
Who can wait for sustenance after so long being famished?
A mirror is an eye that frames a lover's kiss.

Negligee flutters at the thighs, statuesque, a goddess
and her god. Fingernails spark arrows, flinty bed.
A lover is a man who freely shares his bliss,

his arm's cocoon, she swoons to butterfly, metamorphosis.
Who can resist an afternoon of being worshipped?
A mirror is an eye that frames a lover's kiss.

From these heights he is Zeus atop the Acropolis,
her breath a laurel, a sigh of pleasure garlanded.
A lover is a man who freely shares his bliss.

What we give, whom we live for defies analysis.
Carpe diem, bury your ghosts as you bury the dead.
A mirror is an eye that frames a lover's kiss.
A lover is a man who freely shares his fist.

You Can Be That Metaphor

The girl on the back of a scooter
flying by the seat of her pants
down the Rue de Rivoli in Paris,
scarved in pink silk and sequins
and dark, dark sunglasses, hands
squeezed round the fluted waist
of her leatherjacket lover weaving
in and out of traffic, dance of the skirt
as it plays along her thighs.

You can be guided by Paris light,
sluice of gray against grain, melancholy
of his blue eyes over glasses
and glasses of wine. The café
is your sense of time, days measured
in cups of café crème, foam teasing
your lips, until the hum of him
between your legs, driving you
to your destination.

You can be that metaphor:
The hymn of your resurrection
choired in a room with only a bed
and window. There you can be storied
lovers on star-crossed balcony,
his hands cupping your face
as if one could hold the moon
and kiss the light. But this is destiny—
church bells declare it at five
in the morning, accompany you
as you collapse naked, holding each other,
sighing. Only light which touches
the edges of darkness can satisfy—

Paris opens its curtains and listens,
a woman on a balcony opposite
drinks a cup of coffee.
She pretends she doesn't see
the two of you lying there naked
but something in the way she holds
the cup to her mouth for longer
than a sip, eyes narrowing
their focus into your room,
tells you that she, like you, is no
ordinary voyeur, but a connoisseur
of the great escape from middle age
and what it has done to us.

Siesta

After the painting by Pierre Bonnard, 1900

She turns her leg into a question mark as if asking:

Why does lovemaking require a nap afterwards?
Why do the sheets twist themselves into a knot
that cannot be undone as easily as he untangles
her hair from its braid? Why does tea not satisfy
after so many kisses? Why has sugar lost its flavor?

Have they become a taste only one other palate
can recognize? When will he understand
laundering is unnecessary, that to smell him
on the sheets, on her skin, is the perfume
of the pillow, is the tonic that lulls her to sleep.
How can she convince him to seduce her at night?

Why must he always demand daylight?
Why does he say her thighs taste like oranges?
Why is everything a metaphor for color?
Why doesn't he just trace the brush along
the back of her knees, render her useless
for standing, trail his palette knife along the spine,
impress upon the shoulder blade a daub of spice,
color of cinnamon, tattoo of his heart meeting hers?

Why does he say she exhausts him when
he is the one who bolts from bed, leaving
her prone curves to curl alone while he hunches
over the canvas, only to stroke her flesh anew again?

Photografia Digitalis: The Wrecked Bed

What possessed me to do it after he left—
photographing the bed as one would the scene
of a crime? I shot from every angle, a dozen
in all, chronicling the comings and goings
of every orgasm burned into these sheets.
Was I expecting to find marks the size of cigars
or something larger pressed into the flesh
of where I sleep? One paradox of sex—
the heat is always so wet.

First the snap of coral-colored panties flung
on the bedpost, thighs exposed as reefs,
where his fingers had flit like angelfish
skirting the light. Then the zoom lens eyed detail
of the demi-bra draped *in delicato flagranto*
across the lampshade, homage paid to vamp
and vampire, mistress and sire. The quilt,
heartbeat of the sleeping bed, flatlined
against the foot rail. It was dead, no longer
needed here. And the pillows gave up the ghost
of tranquility's hope, jettisoned overboard
as seas were tossed by lovers who only needed
the soft landing of each other.

These were no two ships passing in the night—
It was full-on collision, calamity lifeboat, foghorns
lowering the boom. Here's the evidence to prove
it, or at least the aftermath of a coupling
so titanic the earth really did move,
and the two suspects vanished, swept away
in passion's tidal wave. For how else could the camera
explain this vastness, time and date stamped,
a wrecked bed napless on a Monday afternoon?

Sonnet with Homophones

If the afternoon knows what the morning
never suspected, why not wield the ax,
sever love at the root? Why is mourning
always black resistance, solitary acts

of witness we prefer to hide? The past
is a tight corset worn by heroines
who cannot forget. Whatever passed
between us, those silvered veins, heroin

we mainlined as fever, kiss, the sixth sense,
bliss of the bed and nothing else. It would
be easier to trail you by your scent
than to fell the forest, your heart of wood.

Leave me to what nighttime words always buy:
lesson less than learned, pen poised at goodbye.

The Origami Heart of Winter

There are days winter folds in
upon itself, when mountains grow
a lake and the shoreline bends
a beckoning finger, when the air
is so cold it creases the trees
into icicles. Birds then know it's time
to tuck a wing into a wing, wrap
a feathered cheek against
a similar softness. A nest is made
for two at least, twigs and leaves
and flannel, a weave of aviary
origami. Our bed is threaded
by downy quilt and comfort of near
and nearer still. There's only one
song we hear to keep away the chill.

I've always wanted this kind
of winter: snowflakes stripped
of their spurs, folded into hearts,
curves melting onto tongues,
tucking into kisses one by one.

Loving Icarus

In any light,
you're caramel.
I ask myself—
from what amber
sunset did you
fall?

Your eyes
pull tides
of oceans to life
in my blood.
Each night
the down upon
your arms
turns into wings,
and I build
my nest
between the staves
of your rib cage.

This is how
we will stay
for a long while—
riding each wave,
blowing foam into
glass.

Carpe Diem Love Poem
(Compatible with All Electronic Devices)

Should I drive out tonight, he types, as if
he lived nearby. Six hundred interstate
miles separate, recent storms and snow drifts,
heavy weather complicates, so we date

online. What if Shakespeare had e-mailed
his woo instead of pitching it one line
at a time scrawled on parchment, nailed
to his love's door? *Carpe diem* survives,

interfaces with all electronic
devices. It will have to do, this screen
pixeling my poems, designed to unstick
his heart, make him pack the car, turn the key,

ignite the force of his libido, blast
the carbon from his lungs, come to me, fast.

Poem for the Partially Dressed

*Speak in French when you can't remember the English
for a thing.*

THE RED QUEEN TELLS ALICE

He wrote me he learned a new word: *déshabillé,*
and would I send a picture because it was worth
a thousand somethings. Like I still cared, I said,
to drape myself across a chair and pose with garters
and silk stockings, just to give him a thrill. What's dead
is dead. I didn't have the *coeur* to tell him,
my *sang-froid* had been disrobed, had unshuttered
the lens of someone new who knows *couture*
and photography were invented by the French.
They understand *amour* is an error and armor
is the best defense. Every garment lends fresh proof
to what's askew: no matter who you're with,
love will always undo itself, *embrasser* and tell,
think better of it, and then simply wilt.

Exposure

CAROL STEVENS KNER

Exposure

How can we decide what to keep and what
to give away, what to share and what refuse,
what keep secret, what lay bare? No living thing
slips from the knot of compromise,
not pear tree in prevailing wind
that never finds its perfect ring,
nor vagrant fox that slinks across the field,
nor chipmunk scritching in the wall,
nor phoebes settled on the porch
when we were gone. Brooding now, attached
like buds to stem, too deep to move,
they fret, they flick their tails, they flit from eave
to nest, earnest and plain. We ogle
the small domestic fever of their lives.

Heavenly Rest

Summer lightens everything, beech leaves
that, fallen early, trace the water's flow,
a breeze heavy with scent of new-cut grass,
the stone wall ruffled with vines, the passing
threat of showers, the drift of time, a pool,
and bodies *in flagrante gaudio*.

A man turns slowly, offers to the sun
a belly prospering on bread and wine,
casts a covetous eye on the sublime
thigh, the supple curve of younger flesh
nearby but way beyond his reach, and smiles
at memories. He watches while she oils

each easy-going limb, sees her admire
the sleek sheen of her tan, appear to long
for something that she hasn't got (the blue
bikini in the magazine). Angrily,
she slaps a fly. A woman glances round
and settles back. *This is heaven,* she sighs.

Heaven in this small piece of the universe,
a patch of grass just like the tidy plot
di Paolo painted centuries ago
(*Paradise, a fragment,* in tempera,
the label says), a perfect lawn with trees
that bear ripe golden fruit, and no leaves fall,

where courtiers in fur-edged brocade, a doge,
and wimpled nuns engage in genteel talk.
They all are slim and full of grace, polite,
and never break the rules in deed or thought.
They stroll but never seem to bruise the flowers,
and, clearly, envy does not discompose

the monks because an angel gossips with
the doge. The cavalier does not take pride
in his well-tailored tabard or his red
silk hose. And though the dove of peace appears
to tread air next to the nun's ear, she makes
no move to slap away its noisy wings.

Desire is absent. These blessed souls have
everything. Winter never dims their light,
no shadows fall; there's no perspective here;
no clouds trespass on the eternal sky;
no fears abide, and no one ever weeps
in Paradise. But everyone is dead.

In Memoriam

We breakfast on the splendor of the day,
the meadow's pea-green dazzle, redbird
and goldfinch feeding. Nothing more's required.
      A luna moth displays her pale moiré

against the glass, but she hangs limp like something lynched,
caught by a web and fastened in the gum
of limbo.
      Redeemers with a kitchen broom,
we knock the threads away from the blue-ceilinged porch.

But how unstick the wings? We lay her sorrowful
and shroudless on the grass. Later she has disappeared.
Her fragile, perfectly silent torment's marred
the morning. Some things are impossible.

Let idle talk and the sweet tedium
of summer's noonday drone provide a requiem.

Common Ground

All day we ply this tanglement of woods
where May has roguishly redrawn the map.
Haphazard growth hides blazes now with buds;
slow wreck of fallen pine, washed by the ebb
and flow of fern, clogs an old logging trail;
networks of berry canes conspire to bar
a grassy path; a radiant sun streaked pool
laps at the wounds of an uprooted fir.

Winter's a rude lodger. We tidy up
cut underbrush, shift tumbled trunks, torn
branches, introduce a trace of landscape,
in wilderness of content finding form.
But our small interference won't endure.
It's just a skirmish in an ancient war.

The Visit

Today they have all come for the weekend.
The car is parked, they scatter on the lawn:
Happiness twirling on her painted toes,
Solitude silently clutching his book,
and close behind, Solicitude, who warns
the others off the snaky garden hose.

At lunch, sour Melancholy perches on a stool,
her sodden mantle shading the buffet,
but she's ignored by Bonhomie whose jokes
and family tales garnish the cheese and meats,
while sly Suspicion sniffs the dessert tray
and Self-Absorption fills himself with quiche.

Later, by the lake, the hard edges blur
shimmering in ripples that reflect the light.
It's true that for a spell Pomposity,
blustering along the dock, holds forth
on twine, the binding strength of cotton, hemp,
and nylon sold on skein or cylinder. . . .

The others simply stroll away or swim
until it's time for cocktails on the porch
and someone kindly asks for his advice
about briquettes and how to fire the grill.
Virtue, thank God, takes charge of washing up;
the rest, like children catching fireflies,

saunter noisily to the field where they
pluck constellations from the Milky Way.
After dark, they shuffle off to bed,
except for pallid Romance, who clings fast
to Tedium while he reads the *Times* aloud.
Now Resolution leaves them, shuts the doors,

turns out the lights, lauds the good luck that kept
Decay (her dank grotto of clicking teeth)
at home; lolls with the crossword and a book,
all the day's chatter stopped. And in its place
from discrete rooms throughout the house, only
the uncertain harmony of transient snores.

Masters of the Renaissance

I've heard the Resurrection never was,
that Christ was never buried, never rose
(a caveat prescribed by Roman laws),
His rites the trust of carrion dogs and crows
that preyed on Calvary. Think of the stark
efficiency, the soldiers—a routine
ordeal—the gall; then stinging wind and dark,
and churning earth, the savaged bones picked clean.
But Duccio, Giotto, too, saw Him appear
to Mary on rocky ground, her arms spread
yearning, His warning sharp enough to hear.
Piero saw Him living, the soldiers dead
with drink—the list of witnesses is long:
About history were they ever wrong?

Swimming

Starting up from sleep, shrieking,
you wake me at 4:00 a.m.
I was in a submarine
with the dog, you are saying,
and the windows were breaking.
The water was pouring in.
You were safe. You were staying
somewhere else. I pull you back
to the cup of my body
till I feel your breath slowing,
the cold terror running out,
but we are growing older.
I can't keep the waters from rising.

V.I.P. Lounge

I walk down the corridor of this passenger terminal,
every room a gate to the next destination.
I find my mother studying her passport,
reminding herself over and over
who she was in 1974
when she took her last trip to Europe.
A tied-together pair of new black shoelaces
attaches her passport to my father's.
I don't like that man's picture, she says.
It's square and flat. It doesn't look like him.
I ask if I may close the passports and tie them up.
Yes, she says. *They belong together.*

Stuck into the mahogany frame
of her old bedroom mirror,
where they interrupt her reflection,
are family snapshots.
Accustomed now to the delay in her departure,
she has taken to playing solitaire with them.
She fans them out—a full house
of children and grandchildren.
Flesh and blood, I, too, am familiar,
but she can't place me.

Her brother, his beak-nosed gaze
keeping watch over her blue-chips;
her parents playing Brahms four-hands
on their twin baby grands
are nowhere to be found.

Now she lays the pictures out in rows
and talks to them:
Daddy, shirtless, in his Victory garden
looking into the distance
as if he were thinking up a palindrome;
herself at 40 on a family trip to the Capital,
her head wreathed in cherry blossoms;
my sister and I in snowsuits
lugging an old Christmas tree to the trash;
her grandchildren in formal school portraits.
Lowering her voice so they won't overhear,
she tells me that she can't get them to eat their breakfast.
I, new to the language of this country,
nod as if I understand.

The truth is, I have begun to feel homesick
for my living room where my husband sits reading,
tapping the arm of his chair lightly with his thumb
to the beat of Irish folk music.

In any case, it doesn't matter
whether or not I understand what she says.
I have made arrangements to leave her
under the watchful eye of an interpreter and guide
who will come presently,
bathe her papery skin, and put her to bed.
In the morning, there will be another
to help her up the steep ramp of tomorrow
and every day after that
until it's time for her to leave.

The Edge of Where

We're on the edge of where we used to live.
Her thoughts fly up like crows from old bare
trees. *I used to go with them and give*

them things. Is this the end of childish prayer
"Please keep her safe," her longing for the there
of time gone by, back where she used to live?

Because of all the weather up above,
the people now are mostly women here,
I used to go with them and talk and give

them things. He isn't running anymore.
Can't mend the tatters of her brain or share
the haunted edge of where they used to live.

These trees are different from the ones we have
(the crows, torn banners flapping in the air).
I used to go with them and talk and give—

I'm going home. I'll be so glad to leave.
I've left a good part of myself back there
beyond the edge of where we used to live
when I could go with them and talk and give.

Babblewacky

based on Autopsy Report X-4113,
Albert Einstein College of Medicine,
April 26, 1989

Invisible the senile plaques
that mire and hamper synthesis;
all gluey is the neural flax
entangled in paralysis.

Along the ságittal divide
opaque leptómenínges twine;
the sulci loom especially wide,
the cortical gray mantle's thin.

"Beware gloméruli, my friends,
and amyloid angiopathy!
Beware gliosis and defend
against the gyri's atrophy!"

Powerless here the vorpal blade
to fight the mind's furtive decay.
We cannot amputate the head . . .
nor can the microscope survey

Hirano bodies, ghost neurons,
the neurofibrillary snarl,
the fiendish gimble of the brain—
while body harbors still the soul.

Invisible the senile plaques
growing stealthily like moss,
petrifying layers of chalk,
each tangled gain, another loss.

Of Body and Mind

My love, so far we've managed to escape
life's bleak conspiracies: shipwreck and fire,
money squandered on some desperate hope,
the careless dispatch of a child to war.
But now just as our moon begins to rise,
old currents ruffle up a pirate breeze
that plunders some deep-buried treasure-trove
and fouls your rigging, sets your sails to luff.

For so subversive and malign a scheme,
contrariness will sing louder than blame.
Like maples on the brink of winter's storm,
let's flame red, meddling naysayers disarm,
refuse a passage straitened by regret
for one that's generous and full of light.

Isle of Dogs

SARAH SUZOR

Isle of Dogs

Tiresias, you and I,
we barely know each other.

Take off your jacket, will you?

You say she has obsessions.
You say she can't remember.

These are all things I know.

And what about you?

There's hardly anything to speak of that
hasn't already been mentioned.
Except, of course, how you've been spending your evenings.

Did you tell the experts about that?

I didn't think so.

In Retrospect

It was her obsession with chemistry that got us here.
No, not equations,
the chemistry that occurs
from heat to heat
scent to scent

and now in reaction ...

it was her obsession with the mind,
with motivations,
that got us here.

With merit and Mondays.

It was her obsession with the Atlantic and birds and thunder.

The way lightning sometimes split her vision.

In retrospect, it was her obsession with chemistry.

In Addition To

Earth and sky, two entities.
Between the two forms and four directions of finality,
if ever,
choose beginning and south.
Choose something to aspire to.
There within,
should it be heard,
the song bends the bones.

No frequent gift,
no below zero,
the mountain
deriving such bodies
grants a shadow—
signals morning.

And the wind
bites again,
catches up
to replace remorse.

So do I love her when loose from it.

Not in summation
but in addition to.

Isle of Dogs

Past the Isle of Dogs, eh?

Tiresias,
I have a headache.

I swear, pull this again
and there will be some serious repercussions.

(serious repercussions)

Wander.

Which means no destination.

Which means having no destination.

Which means *fire in the hills*.

Tiresias. I swear.

Cardinal and Capital

Birds and letters.

    Remember all day.

And there continue: estimations.

The experts articulate:
    Lust was originally fornication.
    Originally originated as nothing.

    ◆ ◆ ◆

Not that the birds would never return,
she just held her hand out, waiting all day.

    ◆ ◆ ◆

There continue: strategies—

splits where the road forks—
    she went west,
        of course, I went estimation.

The Isle

Downstream.

Snow on the collar.

Take to directions.

West is just west, and it never runs out.

      ◆ ◆ ◆

The experts say it's where the bodies of dead dogs
wash up on the shore.

The experts have all the rules in the world:

Watch out for a man in an orange jacket.

and

Don't go swimming.

I've taken to directions
and writing down all persons I meet by chance.

Where She Had Been

Violets, blue violets.

The way one always walks downhill first.

She said, I have never been here before.

She had.

The light fell through from breaks in the buildings—
breaks where the sky starts and ends,
and our shadows, uphill behind us.

Where did you go next? I asked.

Again.

I have never been here before.

     ◆   ◆   ◆

From what I could tell
there were two types and four directions

but with the situation being circumstantial,
and the circumstances coincidental,
the principal agent became sunlight.

The catalyst: wings.

Where She Went Next

An easy thought of silence
where truth comes in two forms:

finality and acceptance.

Acceptance is the beginning again.

Finality, just that.

She has made it impossible,
as I am made without wings.

Impossible autumn
letting loose its rain,
its catharsis,
its misleading security.

     ◆ ◆ ◆

But to strategize the estimate:

Two types,
four directions,
and three questions.

What really matters is memory,
call it,
in this instance,
a catalyst.
What really matters now is skin.

     ◆ ◆ ◆

Incessant whistling
and always the wind.
It must be her but younger,
her, but decision,
her, but only two answers to every question.
Two types.

Incessant answers and paper on fire.
It must be a catalyst,
no, the wind.

◆ ◆ ◆

QUESTION 1:

Which is the season for returning?

Indeed
the Divide does look lovely.

Immediate autumn.

What a good whistler she was.

The truth is Cardinals don't whistle,
the truth is originally originated as nothing.

There are no Cardinal truths,
no Capital letters,

the experts articulate.

◆ ◆ ◆

QUESTION 2:

Which is the scent of spring?

The catalyst and on and on,
or thick air wet with rainwater.

I have run into her remarkably
remembering all day,
skin swollen with coincidence,
tongue whistling.

Embodied as a bird

she is a better half.

A double-winged wonder.

◆ ◆ ◆

QUESTION 3:

Is fire a matter of flint and stone?

If so,
wildflowers.

Indeed the Divide does cast its division.
A shadow—
east on Friday
west on Wednesday,
all a matter of ordinary,
a matter of high noon.

Consume

Two sides to every coin,
and there continue: adages.

I am consumed by it,

and this skeleton,
if there was ever room to invade.

     ❖ ❖ ❖

The experts have two rules:

When something is distracting concentrate on its shadow.

and

Never open the match-box upside down.

     ❖ ❖ ❖

From what I could tell
she had hollow bones,
those of a bird.
From what I could tell
the principal agent originated from
an impending prediction of loss.

The catalyst: silence.

In Seclusion

I expect to think of skeletons and blue violets.

I expect my reflections to lead me to a point of remembering.

Nothing of the sea. I tell myself
nothing of the sea.

And then: antidotes.

The sound of melancholy and catharsis.
Rain on the roof.

From what I understand it's where the bodies of dead dogs
wash up on the shore.

From what I understand it's a place for forgetting.

The security is catharsis,
misleading rain.
The security is seclusion in an orange jacket.

Water Like This

It's not easy these days,
and it's nowhere near the moment she's been waiting for.

But it is the Atlantic,
the Atlantic in August,
and since then
I have held her in all my dreams.

No one knows which is worse:

walking into the ocean alone
or walking into the ocean in general.

The beginning again or the finality.

The agent or catalyst.

The ordinary or the exceptional.

In retrospect, it was her obsession with answers that got us here.

Isle of Dogs

Fire in the hills, eh?
That's actually very funny.

She's told me she watches the waves breaking
their backs at the shore.
They have backs, she says,
and enter into themselves
hour after hour
only so one knows this moment
is not the same as the last.

It's heartbreaking, really.

But Tiresias, I don't expect you to understand.

Sightlines

MOLLY PEACOCK

The poets collected here under a single title, *Sightline*, form a felic-
itous quartet: four voices combining to deliver a deliciously eccen-
tric but harmonious single book of poems. One could even think
of these voices as the instruments of a string quartet: two violins,
a viola, and a cello. And one could go even further in listening to
them as the four *movements* in a quartet. Four players and four
instruments working four overlapping themes, remarkably cohe-
sive considering that each movement has been created by a differ-
ent composer. The poets are all impressively deft with their craft.
Each of them rejects the oversimplified and embraces—with
elegance—her complex interpretation of the world. They are all
worth reading and re-reading—or, to keep the musical metaphor in
mind, listening to, again and again.

We begin with *Where Currents Meet* by **Elizabeth Austen**,
whose poem "It Didn't Happen That Way" reconfigures the story
of Adam and Eve. In Austen's version, Adam pries the fruit from
Eve's hand, inverting their traditional roles, and this act provokes
the issues of womanhood that Austen explores throughout this
opening sequence. In her sonnet "Goodbye My Millions" those mil-
lions are not monetary currency, but biological: eggs contained in
the ovaries of a female foetus. "I know / you can't help it—your
nature to ripen / and leap." Biology sets up the reader for essential
questions: what is human nature and, more importantly for those
Eves who hold the fruit of their intuitions in their hands, what is
human about a woman's social self, that self which must respond
not to its nature and intuition (and by extension, art) but to its obli-
gations? Austen's intense sequence of poems grapples with this,
wrestling with full poetic muscle. She begins with a sense of "The
Permanent Fragility of Meaning" and states, "I lie down in the
dark. / I rise up and begin again." Her poem "Humans" is written
just at the nexus of social obligation and the desire to simply be. Is
simple being possible, Austen seems to ask, turning to nature for
answers in "False Spring" and "Shi Shi Beach." She closes her ambi-
tious sequence with acceptance. "You could wait your whole / life
for sense to take shape." Refusing to be stymied, the poet's

determined last words are "Keep looking." That command becomes an anthem both for the speaker of this work and the work of the writers who follow.

Andrea Bates introduces an aphoristic buoyancy into the second movement of this four-part composition, *Origami Heart*. "Love is eternal while it lasts," she quips in "L'Amour Fou, L'Amour Wild." With humor, charm and enticing vocabulary, she gives us an ingenious villanelle, "View from a Mirror: Couple Kissing," after a photograph by Brassai. "Who can resist an afternoon of being worshipped?" she sighs in the middle, then twists the lyric to surprise violence at the end. Full of mirrors and windows, Bates's poems offer the romantic point of view from a multitude of clever angles created by oddball questions. In "Siesta" she asks whimsically, "Why does love-making require a nap afterwards?" And in "*Photografia Digitalis:* The Wrecked Bed," the speaker dares to inquire, "What possessed me to do it after he left— / photographing the bed as one would the scene / of a crime?" Sometimes ekphrasis is her mode, the poems evoking photography and the painting of Bonnard. Sometimes she boldly kidnaps formal conventions for her purposes with invigorating cleverness, such as in her "Sonnet with Homophones," in which "acts" rhymes with "ax," "heroines" with "heroin," and "would" with "wood." This precedes her painterly title poem, "The Origami Heart of Winter." Her formal panache resurfaces in her penultimate poem, a sonnet called "*Carpe Diem* Love Poem (Compatible with All Electronic Devices)." "What if Shakespeare had e-mailed / his woo . . . / *Carpe diem* survives, // interfaces with all electronic / devices." Bates's high-flying sequence ends with "Poem for the Partially Dressed" evoking Robert Herrick's "sweet disorder in the dress" with her intimate, gossipy profundity. "Every garment lends fresh proof / to what's askew." Who can resist someone who takes on so much, so lightly, yet with such intensity, and all the while having so much fun?

Sarah Suzor makes snappy interrogations of Tiresias, the blind seer of Thebes who famously revealed to Oedipus that Oedipus had murdered his father. But another aspect of Tiresias's story, used by T.S. Eliot in "The Wasteland," is that the prophet spent seven years of his life as a woman, transgendered by Hera's vengeance. Suzor's speaker talks to Tiresias, who becomes a pal, an intimate to be yelled at and confided in, an older friend. What's under discussion with the revivified ancient seer is the course of a relationship, the ups and downs between the speaker of the poems and a lover. "There continue strategies—" Suzor explains in "Cardinal and Capital," and she goes on to describe "splits where the road forks— / she went west, / of course, I went estimation." Marvelously sharp and plucky-voiced, the poems pose question after question, echoing a similar question approach in Bates's poems, reinforcing that musical idea of the quarter, themes from a second movement appearing, changed to different purposes, in another. "Where She Went Next" presses on absurdity, braiding question with question on the subject of love's exasperations.

Suzor's poems borrow lines back and forth from one another until, through their play, a wry acceptance is reached. "No one knows which is worse:" she states in "Water Like This," "walking into the ocean alone / or walking into the ocean in general. / The beginning again or the finality. / The agent or the catalyst. / The ordinary or the exceptional. / In retrospect, it was her obsession with answers that got us here." Titles and locales surface in the poems with piquant frequency, until the "Isle of Dogs," the title of the final poem, but also of the first poem and the fourth, reverberates into a finale. (The Isle of Dogs here is a mythical, suggestive name, though the actual Isle of Dogs is a former island that is now part of London's East End where Canary Wharf is located.) In the ongoing musical instrumentation of this book, Suzor's voice becomes the viola, darkening the themes that Austen and Bates introduced.

The anchoring depth of this quartet is provided by the cello-like voice of the poems of **Carol Stevens Kner**. Her title poem, "Exposure," states the theme of her sequence with elegant lucidity. "No living thing / slips from the knot of compromise." Kner proceeds to unravel the knot of compromise with each work in the sequence. Experience has been her teacher, and she becomes ours, writing from an earned perspective. From this vantage point she is able to tell us, in "Common Ground," "But our small interference won't endure. / It's just a skirmish in an ancient war." Kner makes domestic and romantic observations with the alluringly contradictory combination of a cool eye and loving engagement. Her passionate distance allows a deftness of craft (like Bates, she makes the sonnet sing). "Swimming" is piercingly intelligent and moving. With both heat and empathy Kner invokes a middle-of-the-night scene when a husband wakes to relate a bad dream while the wife comforts, building the poem with the quiet chill of foreboding. In "V.I.P. Lounge" (V.I.P. is all too close to R.I.P. here) Kner provokes thoughts of ageing and "the steep ramp of tomorrow." Candor and clarity are her hallmarks. These poems create a steady light all their own, like light from a north-facing window. With a full range of emotions, the steadiness of her stance allows her to evoke a variety of states of mind. Her villanelle "Babblewacky" about just these states brilliantly fuses the prosody of Lewis Carroll's "Jabberwocky" with the psychobiology of senility: "the neurofibrillary snarl, / the fiendish gimble of the brain." She revives that almost abandoned technique of personification, where, with warmth and perspective but without a shred of sentiment, she creates characters of Happiness, Solitude, Melancholy, Self-Absorption, Suspicion and Pomposity, all arrived for a summer weekend in "The Visit." Kner's subjects are both the end of life and the source of poetry itself: the inextricable combination of love and loss that beats inside human experience.

Rich in thought, sentiment, and craft, *Sightline* is also rich in those two essential subjects of poetry, love and loss. As the cello's voice contrasts and merges with the voices of the two distinct violins and the viola in a string quartet, so this quartet of poets, Elizabeth Austen, Andrea Bates, Carol Stevens Kner, and Sarah Suzor, acquires its opulence from the gift of each individual balancing in dynamic poise with the gifts of the others.

Molly Peacock
Toronto, Ontario 2010

Notes

About the Authors

AUSTEN: "The Permanent Fragility of Meaning": The title is taken from Jacques Attali's *Noise: The Political Economy of Music* (University of Minnesota Press, 1985).

"Her, at Two" owes its beginning to Grace Rothmeyer, Sharon Olds and Langston Hughes' poem "Luck."

"Where Currents Meet": Cattle Point, at the southwestern edge of San Juan Island in Washington State, is subject to strong currents where flows from Haro Strait and the San Juan Channel mingle.

Elizabeth dedicates *Where Currents Meet* to her parents, Phil and Pat.

KNER: The author would like to thank the Ragdale Foundation for the support which allowed her to complete this manuscript, and Molly Peacock for her encouragement and generosity.

"Heavenly Rest": stanza 4, line 3 refers to Giovanni di Paolo di Grazia (active 1417, died 1482).

"Babblewacky" is for Laura Brandt Stevens.

SUZOR: "In Addition To": *So do I love her when loose from it* is from Canto 2 of Dante's *Purgatorio*.

ABOUT THE AUTHORS

ELIZABETH AUSTEN is the author of a chapbook, *The Girl Who Goes Alone* (Floating Bridge Press, 2010). You can hear her author interviews and poetry commentary at Seattle's NPR affiliate KUOW.org. She has received grants from the City of Seattle Office of Arts and Culture and 4Culture, and is an alumna of Artsmith, Hedgebrook and The Helen Riaboff Whiteley Center. More information at elizabethausten.org.

ANDREA BATES's poems have appeared in *The Wanderlust Review, Bloodroot, Main Street Rag, Common Ground Review* and other journals. She was the 2010 winner of the North Carolina Poetry Society Thomas H. McDill award. She holds a BA from The University of Massachusetts-Amherst, and an MAW from Manhattanville College. Originally from Connecticut, Bates has called Wilmington, NC home since 2001. She teaches writing and literature at community colleges.

CAROL STEVENS KNER has written articles for the *Encyclopedia of World Art, Connaissance des Arts* and the *New Book of Knowledge* and served for many years as managing editor and staff writer at PRINT Magazine; she left that publication to write poems. Her work has appeared in *Western Humanities Review, The Paris Review, North American Review, Connecticut River Review* and *Southwest Review*. She lives in New York City with Andrew Kner, her husband of 49 years.

SARAH SUZOR is the author of *It was the season, then* (EtherDome Chapbooks, 2010). Her poetry, reviews and interviews have appeared in online and print journals including *OR, Tarpaulin Sky* and *Rain Taxi*. Her manuscript, *The Principle Agent,* will be published by Black Lawrence Press in 2011. She lives in Los Angeles, where she is an editor for Highway 101 Press and a visiting lecturer at the Left Bank Writers' Retreat.

Toadlily Press is committed to preserving ancient forests and natural resources. We elected to print this title on 30% post-consumer recycled paper, processed chlorine-free. As a result, for this printing, we have saved:

1 Tree (40' tall and 6-8" diameter)
506 Gallons of Wastewater
1 million BTUs of Total Energy
31 Pounds of Solid Waste
105 Pounds of Greenhouse Gases

Toadlily Press made this paper choice because our printer, Thomson-Shore, Inc., is a member of Green Press Initiative, a nonprofit program dedicated to supporting authors, publishers, and suppliers in their efforts to reduce their use of fiber obtained from endangered forests.

For more information, visit www.greenpressinitiative.org

Environmental impact estimates were made using the Environmental Defense Paper Calculator. For more information visit: www.edf.org/papercalculator

Sightline was composed in Sabon, a typeface designed in 1967 at Linotype by Jan Tschichold. The type family—a classic, elegant and highly legible book face—is based on the work of Claude Garamond and his pupil Jacques Sabon.

ABOUT THE PRESS

Every title in the *Quartet Series* presents four poets—each represented by a chapbook in one perfect-bound volume. Toadlily Press offers poets an opportunity to "converse" with each other, and we hope our readers experience the harmonies and counterpoints as well.

TOADLILY TITLES

2010   SIGHTLINE
Elizabeth Austen, Andrea Bates, Carol Stevens Kner, Sarah Suzor

2009   BY WAY OF
Diana Alvarez, Emily Carr, Matthew Nienow, Diana Woodcock

2008   AN UNCOMMON ACCORD
Marcia Arrieta, Michael Carman, Pat Landreth Keller,
George Kraus

2007   EDGE BY EDGE
Emma Bolden, Gladys Justin Carr, Heidi Hart (includes her
Pushcart Prize winning poem, "Door Psalm," reprinted in
volume XXXIII: Best of the Small Presses 2009), Vivian Teter

2006   THE FIFTH VOICE
Victoria Givotovsky, Pamela Hart, Noah Kucij, Allen Strous

2005   DESIRE PATH
Myrna Goodman, Maxine Silverman, Meredith Trede,
Jennifer Wallace